Travelers on My Route

For Ethan Nghia, Newly Arrived

The final seven
days of every year, the jolly

Earth Spirit
must deliver the state-of-the-world report

to the Jade Emperor
of Heaven. This year he'll mention you,

and he will try,
with difficulty, to describe

the soft new light
that glows behind your mother's face.

Unrecorded

We breathe in smoke when Pepys describes the fire
of London, wince when Plath bites Hughes's cheek
at their intense encounter. As sirens shriek
to celebrate the dying of the war,
Virginia Woolf's transcription draws us there.
The journal is a compass that can take
coordinates of triumph or of heartache,
then point the poet to a vein of ore.

But my days lodge on unmarked streets, at home
to travelers on my route. The ordered saving
of every hour's chatter, doubt, and crumb
would stamp the faded silk of memory's weaving.
It's heresy, but no: there is no room
to chronicle a life consumed with living.

Wake and Stretch

Al Dente

Dinner with Empress Livia	49
Detto	51
The Day Verrocchio Put His Paintbrush Down	52
The Perfect Gentleman	54
Water Games	55
Tour Guide's Lament	57

Like Wingless Birds

A Modest Proposal	61
The Whole Truth	62
Judgment	63
The Battered Wife	64
Turquoise Anita on the Dance Floor	65
Waiting for the Open Air in a Time of Covid	68

Staccato of the Cane

At Home When Old	71
Mind to Body	72
Cane People	73
My Last School Reunion	74
Traveling	75
The Club	76
Let-Down	77
While You're Away	78
Being Read To	79
Metamorphosis	80

Contents

Wake and Stretch

Unrecorded	15
For Ethan Nghia, Newly Arrived	16
End-of-Summer's Cricket Serenade	17
A Calendar of Trees	18
First Birthday	20
The Loser	21

Time's Fingerprints

The Dining Room Wallpaper	25
The Blue Bathtub	26
The Kiss	27
A Note from Mrs. B, My Son's First-Grade Teacher	28
Cat-Tale	29
Wedding Day	30
Mother-in-Law	31
Taking the Chairs Away	32
Dear Ladies	33
Occasional Poems for My Husband	34

Glow

Loving the Work of Hateful Men	37
Waltzing with Wendy	38
Stephanie Dancing	39
The Robin Hour	40
Verbs I Learned at the Opera	41
Rapture	43
Poetry Isn't	44
At the Poetry Retreat	45

Anthologies:

Corona: An Anthology of Poems, ed. Gayl Teller (Walt Whitman Birthplace Association, 2020): "At Home When Old"

Paumanok: Transition, ed. Kathaleen Donnelly (Island Sound Press, 2022): "Rainbow Nails" (reprinted from *Grandma Poems—Not Too Sweet* by Carolyn Raphael, Kelsay Books, 2017), "Taking the Chairs Away"

I would like to thank several friends, teachers, and colleagues for their invaluable help with my poetry: Rhina P. Espaillat, who was never too busy to write discerning critiques; Suzanne Noguere, for her generous time and editor's eye; and Arthur Mortensen, who has always supported my work. I also want to thank several poets whose insights have refined my poems over the years: Annie Finch, R.S. Gwynn, X. J. Kennedy, Charles Martin, Molly Peacock, Timothy Steele, and Marilyn Taylor. My deepest appreciation goes to my phonetician-husband Larry, for his ever-patient reading and listening.

Acknowledgments

I want to thank the editors of the publications in which the following poems, or earlier versions of them, first appeared:

Blue Unicorn: "Loving the Work of Hateful Men," "A Modest Proposal"

Cumberland Poetry Review: "Mother-in-Law," "Metamorphosis"

Expansive Poetry Online: "A Calendar of Trees," "A Note from Mrs. B, My Son's First-Grade Teacher," "At the Poetry Retreat," "Cat-Tale," "Dinner with Empress Livia," "End-of-Summer's Cricket Serenade," "Rapture," "The Battered Wife," "The Perfect Gentleman," "The Whole Truth," "Traveling," "Waiting for the Open Air in a Time of Covid," "Waltzing with Wendy"

Iambs & Trochees: "Unrecorded"

Life and Legends: "First Birthday," "Water Games"

Long Island Quarterly: "My Last School Reunion," "Turquoise Anita on the Dance Floor"

Mezzo Cammin: "Stephanie Dancing," "While You're Away"

Nassau County Poet Laureate Society Review: "Cane People," "Dear Ladies," "Poetry Isn't," "The Dining Room Wallpaper," "Judgment"

Oberon: "Tour Guide's Lament"

For my family—
Larry, Melissa, Frank, Andrew, Gabriel,
David, Nina, Nathan, Benjamin, Rae

© 2023 Carolyn Raphael. All rights reserved.
This material may not be reproduced in any form, published,
reprinted, recorded, performed, broadcast,
rewritten, or redistributed without
the explicit permission of Carolyn Raphael.
All such actions are strictly prohibited by law.

Cover design by Shay Culligan
Cover image by Ray Chan via Unsplash
Author photograph by Larry Raphael

ISBN: 978-1-63980-252-4

Kelsay Books
502 South 1040 East, A-119
American Fork, Utah 84003
Kelsaybooks.com

Travelers on My Route

Poems by

Carolyn Raphael

End-of-Summer's Cricket Serenade

I raise my bedroom window every night
to hear the crickets trill a lullaby.
The synchronous male voices glorify
the power of their prowess to excite.
The females chirp a short response, invite
their suitors to persist and amplify.
They choose the sweetest love song, then they fly
to one whose presentation brings delight.

New word: I learned that crickets stridulate
their song, and not by rubbing legs but wings.
In heat they carol at a faster rate.
You might ask why I care about such things.
My answer is they help me meditate
on letting go, and on the peace it brings.

A Calendar of Trees

1. American Holly

The whole tree shakes, alive with gorging,
as catbirds seize the ripe red berries.
It lasts for hours, each December.
I gaze through my window—entranced, unnerved
by this hibernal sacrifice.
A final shudder, berries are gone,
and stillness returns to spiny leaves
that wait, with evergreen grit, for winter.

2. Japanese Maple

All winter, leafless branches bend
like dancers arcing to the floor.
Strangely, their weeping makes me smile.
Buds swell, then leaflets rise in spring,
slowly unfurl their lacy leaves
until they form a crimson dome.
I look down from an upstairs window
to see the tree nymph wake and stretch.

3. White Pine

Nature's Christmas tree off-season
is out of place in this summer air.
An outsized guest in my small backyard—
the British kings used them for masts.
Some needles yellow, then turn to brown
and fall each fall. I think it's dying,
but it's only pruning the weak and old,
making way for the newly green.

4. American Sweetgum

Each fall I curse this lofty tree
as I turn my ankle on the fallen pods—
fierce as a medieval mace,
big as golf balls and prickly sharp
until leaf blowers blast them away.
But then the leaves—five-pointed stars—
turn yellow, purple, red against
an azure sky, and I forgive.

First Birthday

For Peter Chetta

Today the birthday melody is flat—
the gifts, bouquets of flowers on his grave.
Each guest puts on a coal-black party hat,
and no one knows the right way to behave.

He would have marked his 80th year this day,
but we will have to carry on without him.
We'll raise a glass to friendship anyway,
exchanging famous anecdotes about him.

He bought three kinds of cakes (the ones on sale)
on Wednesdays for the lower seniors' rate,
recalled each play he saw in full detail:
the theater, stars, the usher, and the date.

We smile, then note his absence from our table;
we celebrate his life, as we are able.

The Loser

Abandoned in bathrooms,
restaurants, hotel rooms;
left on buses and trains.
Donations to the world.

I picture a woman dressed
in my losings.
She stands smiling in the rain
in my polka dot poncho,
wearing a twisted gold earring,
rings on four fingers,
broken-in sneakers,
mismatched leather gloves,
a long silk scarf with
black-and-white magnolias.

Who will find my last gift,
my life? A dozen people raise
my umbrellas to the sky,
toasting my largesse.

Time's Fingerprints

The Dining Room Wallpaper

It came with the house:
a tenant who just wouldn't leave.
Thin vertical stripes (Colonial Red on cream),
tiny tulips, chevrons, circles.
My heirloom,
never to be passed down.

Fifty years on the wall
and still holding,
clean from disuse
except for some smudges
near the switchplate—
time's fingerprints.

Friends were surprised
that I didn't repaper the room
to stamp my ownership.
But I like continuity:
conversation and candles,
wine glasses and laughter,
food too good
to eat in the kitchen.
Overseen by Colonial stripes.

The Blue Bathtub

Rip out everything, the plumber snarled.
I countered: *Ravager of history—*
this bathroom is 84 years old,
just a year older than my husband,
and I'm keeping him.
Look at that royal blue bathtub,
porcelain over cast iron,
long enough to stretch out your legs.
Note the delicate blues
of the little square floor tiles,
the four-inch, dove-gray wall tiles
edged in the same electric blue.
New grouting makes them glow again.
Of course the shower is a trial:
I need a washcloth to turn it off.
And the old pipes may give out any day—
but, then again, so may mine.
I bathed my three- and six-year-old children
together in this tub.
With their hair in suds, they looked alike,
though boy and girl, with different skin tones.
I had to replace the royal blue toilet
and matching pedestal sink,
but the bathtub still reigns.
The next owners will surely remodel,
but I'll never see that.
Meanwhile, this tub is my diary,
photograph album, memory bank.
Rip it out indeed!
Just clear the drain in the bathtub, Marco.

The Kiss

My three-year-old is iced
with chocolate pudding,
forehead to chin,
puckered to kiss
his grandma,
who bends down to be frosted.

Not an instant's hesitation.
An offer like this must not be
refused or modified.
Though no one photographed
the transfer,
her willingness was all.

A Note from Mrs. B,
My Son's First-Grade Teacher

> *David had a bad day today.*
> *He couldn't stay seated*
> *or keep his hands to himself.*

I know your many students clamor for
your eyes, your ears, your time (in short supply),
but did you ask our son what troubled him,
what goaded him to lose his self-control?

> *When I told him I would have to*
> *write to you, he told me that he hoped*
> *I would hurt myself.*

I wish that you had chosen to call or write
to us directly, not to tell our son
that you would *have* to write to us. He must
have felt attacked and used his weapon: words.

I was bewildered by your stationery
that shows a smiling teacher holding a big
red apple! And printed in boldface on the top:
An apple from your teacher.

I'll call the office so that we can meet.
We'll bring our listening ears—but not an apple.

Cat-Tale

Crouched beneath an orange moon,
a cat—unclean and thin—
was rescued by a gentle girl,
who gladly took her in.

The savior was Melissa Kay,
in need of an ally
to listen to her discontents
and give a soft reply.

Melissa urged the cat to mew
with milk and cans of tuna;
she even sent a feline prayer
up to the goddess Luna.

The goddess granted her request,
and when the new moon rose,
the cat awakened from her nap,
striking a haughty pose.

Catbird, she said, *catwalk, catarrh,
catnip,* and *catalog.*
Melissa seized her new smartphone
to post this on her blog.

Catcall, the orator declaimed,
cat house and *caterwaul.*
That's quite enough, Melissa said.
There's a shelter at the mall.

Next time you're walking past the stores,
for exercise or shopping,
beware of any cat you see—
and don't consider stopping.

Wedding Day

For Melissa and Frank
October 7, 2001

The stage is placed near maple, oak, and pine—
white bows set out to celebrate the way.
A trellised arch weaves berries and grapevine;
the flag is raised for a performance day.
Ten months of labor have produced this birth—
attended by dressmaker, florist, printer.
The families congregate to see brought forth
an eager groom, a bride about to enter.

Beneath fall's canopy of red and gold,
the guests arrive in dresses, gowns, and suits.
Huddling with friends or blankets (it is cold),
they check the sight lines and reserve their seats.
The quartet having tuned, the violin
gives a decisive nod, and we begin.

Mother-in-Law

The day our daughter walked the aisle,
then, suddenly, became a wife,
her father grew an in-law's smile;
her groom put on a husband's life.

But I, who didn't swear a vow,
offend a goddess, snub a god,
was metamorphosed anyhow
into a comic lightning rod.

I tried to find a liberal ear
and beg a hearing for my plea
to make this jester disappear,
restoring the authentic me.

But now I know the ear is mine,
that soon a lesson will be learned
because affection can define
new kinship—not enforced but earned.

Taking the Chairs Away

I actually liked my mother-in-law.
A gracious hostess, she
placed doilies under grapefruit,
warmed dinner plates in the oven.
At her dining room table six chairs
reigned since her wedding in 1928.
Vaguely Chippendale with oak frames,
the seats were uniformed in moss-green stripes.
When she moved, we sold the table
and the four side chairs,
but no one wanted the armchairs
since one was broken.
We left them outside,
legs forced into a snowbank.
Watching the garbage men
toss them into the truck,
I wished for a ritual.
Also discarded were dinners that lingered
over marble cake and coffee,
evenings without TV or cellphones,
dishes that had to be washed by hand.

Dear Ladies

Our staff is celebrated for its patient and devoted care.
Only a family member can give more.
                    —Garden Nursing Home

Please turn her gently—yes, the sores are healed,
but since her skin tears at the slightest pull,
you'll need the lotion that the doctor ordered.
She relished steamy bowls of chicken soup,
fat turkeys served with ground fresh cranberry sauce.
She's having trouble swallowing, so now
her food must all be ground. A smile from you
would be like music at the dinner hour.
Her eyes will thank you since her words are gone.
Those eyes, not brown like mine but smoky blue
with flecks of yellow like a cat's. They tell
amusement, boredom, fear, or pain—you'll know.
Oh yes, and lipstick. My mother wouldn't take
out garbage without color on her lips,
so please apply the coral that I left.
And one last favor, ladies, if you would—
there's a glass bead necklace in the second drawer
and matching earrings for the holidays.

Occasional Poems for My Husband

1. Anniversary Wishes in Germany

Not Italy for us, this year, my dear—
we'll venture north to see the Pergamon Gate.
We'll say a word in Nefertiti's ear,
and guzzle Pilsner at a daunting rate.

We'll leave a stone in Weimar and Berlin;
we'll pause where Schiller and great Goethe versed.
We know there'll be no pappardelle in
the brauhaus or café. (It could be wurst.)

2. Birthday Wishes in the Time of Covid

No trip this year—alas, alack.
The Met will not be coming back;
the other Mets are off the track
(and I'm accumulating plaque).

According to the almanac,
today's your birthday; let's attack
a solo party with your knack
for building a banquet from a snack.

Glow

Loving the Work of Hateful Men

I won't renounce the gold of Dickens' *Bleak House*,
the heat of *Die Walküre*'s "Spring Song" blaze,
the decadence of Caravaggio's *Bacchus*,
his dirty fingernails and wanton gaze.

But what about the heart and hands that shaped
the words, the song, the pigment into life?
Are they exempt from rules of decency?
Allowed to foment hate, abuse a wife?

How can we part the artist from the craft?
Admire the oleander bloom but shun
the poison leaves? At what cost compromise?
A deft maneuver, but it can be done.

If I convince myself that notes display
no malice, that prose or paintings can be built
to elevate above a flawed foundation,
perhaps I can embrace them free of guilt.

Waltzing with Wendy

On October 18, 2014, two renowned New York City Ballet dancers, Jacques d'Amboise and Wendy Whelan, briefly waltzed together on the stage after her farewell performance. (She had lived with his family when a student at the School of American Ballet.) D'Amboise, when he joined Wendy in this waltz, was 80 years old.

A slow run to meet him, a loving embrace.
He gives her a rose, then they walk to the place
where flowers are piled in tribute. (His gait
is measured and cautious—we worry and wait.)
The applause turns to shouts as she donates his rose.
Another embrace—he whispers—she knows.
They waltz—here's the infinite grace I recall
from the king of the leap and the lift (and so tall).
He changes direction—crescendo of cheers.
He twirls her, a last hug, and we are in tears.

Stephanie Dancing

For Stephanie Davis

She moved through air and made it glow—
her body chronicled the joy.
When music beckoned, fast or slow,
she moved through air and made it glow.

The lucky ones who watched her know
the grace that time could not destroy.
She moved through air and made it glow;
her body chronicled the joy.

The Robin Hour

For Amy Finkston, artist

Fat-bellied robins attack my American Holly,
fill their beaks with red berries,
orange breast feathers puffed
against the cold.
They race across my yard then land
on the evergreen leaves, avoiding,
somehow, their spiny teeth.

It's a collage, ready to assemble.
Look out my window; stop the action
as you play with the shapes and colors.
Leave us one more memory
before you slip away, smiling.

Verbs I Learned at the Opera

How to learn Italian verbs—
not from drills *(parlo, parli, parla)*
or classroom conversation,
when I freeze until
I find some notes to lean on.
I need inducement, something I love
to beckon me into *la lingua italiana*.
And I know what it is: opera.

I never forget the conditional tense
when Mozart's Zerlina sings
Vorrei e non vorrei,
tempted by irresistible Don Giovanni.
Or the passato remoto of Tosca's prayer:
Vissi d'arte, vissi d'amore.
The imperative of *bere* glows like Merlot
in Iago's drinking song
Beva con me from Verdi's *Otello*.

But I can remember the verbs
only in operatic contexts.
How often will I have the chance to say
in the imperative:
Ritorna vincitor!
as Aida says to Radames,
betraying her father?
Or in the future tense,
Non più andrai, farfallone amoroso
when Figaro teases Cherubino
in *Le Nozze di Figaro?*

Actually, there were two occasions
that demanded verbs from operas.
When I tired of telling my son to put on his jacket,

I tried *Vesti la giubba*,
which Canio says sadly to his mirror
as he dresses to become the smiling clown
in *Pagliacci*.
Then there was my declaration.
Once a week, in a loud voice, I chanted
Nessun dorma,
Puccini's famous aria from *Turandot*,
when I wanted my children to
straighten their rooms before bed.
An unwelcome reminder—but it was imperative.

I'll keep looking for ways to use libretto Italian
in my quest to be fluent.
As I trudge ahead,
sounding like a fourth grader,
I dream of my husband crooning,
on a cold night (in a sweet imperative),
Che gelida manina, se la lasci riscaldar
from *La Bohème*.
I respond *Sì* without hesitation.
And he does.

Translations

Vorrei e non vorrei	I would like to and I would not
Vissi d'arte, vissi d'amore	I lived for art; I lived for love
Beva con me	Drink with me
Ritorna vincitor!	Return a conqueror
Non più andrai, farfallone amoroso	No more will you go, amorous butterfly
Vesti la giubba	Put on your costume
Nessun dorma	No one shall sleep
Che gelida manina, se la lasci riscaldar	What a frozen little hand; let me warm it for you

Rapture

On watching then 11-year-old Israeli violinist Masha Mershon play the "Meditation" solo from Massenet's opera Thaïs *with the Israel Philharmonic Orchestra conducted by Roni Porat.*

Eyes closed, lips slightly parted, Masha plays
the lovely Intermezzo from *Thaïs*.
Transported, where? Where does a young girl go?
From time to time she opens her eyes, looks briefly
at the conductor, resumes the sweet refrain.
Unlike Thaïs, viewing the afterlife,
the violinist honors this one, onstage,
stroking the notes that lullaby her soul.
Eyes closed, she sounds the high harmonic note
that brings the traveler home, reluctantly.

Poetry Isn't

Poetry isn't
soft (as a swansdown powder puff)
stale (as a bolt from the blue)
manifest (as a cleaver hacks meat)

It's
facewhacking
brightpenny
new

At the Poetry Retreat

I sleep in a nun's bed—reflection begins.
I gaze at the Bible, the sunlight, the sea;
then I put on my makeup and ponder my sins.

First, Gluttony leads me to gorge on Rice Thins,
which I eat without guilt since they're now gluten-free.
I sleep in a nun's bed—reflection begins.

An arrow from Eros (I yield as he grins),
but Sloth neuters Lust; I am saved from a spree.
Still, I put on my makeup and ponder my sins.

When Envy and Greed vie, I hear violins
that solemnly practice my soul's threnody.
I sleep in a nun's bed—reflection begins.

Engaged in a battle where nobody wins—
I rail against Wrath (to a modest degree)
while putting on makeup, pondering sins.

I stare in the mirror at Lucifer's twins:
the dragons of Pride and Vanity.
I sleep in a nun's bed—reflection begins
as I pile on makeup and ponder my sins.

Al Dente

Dinner with Empress Livia

Livia Drusilla (later Julia Augusta) was the third wife of Emperor Augustus. She lived from 58 BCE to 29 CE. Her Prima Porta Villa's beautiful dining room frescoes were moved to Rome's Palazzo Massimo al Terme (Roman National Museum) in 1998. Today, one can sit surrounded by garden scenes of flowers and fruit trees filled with doves and partridges. And dream.

Cornelius to Lucius, Greetings

I must describe my dinner with our Empress.
Her sprawling, lavish villa outshines praise.
One marvel is the summer dining room:
partially underground, the perfect place
to flee the ravages of Roman heat.
High up, small windows let in just enough light.

On all four walls the artist painted frescoes
that echo the surroundings of this villa.
Cerulean blue and beryl green assuage
the troubled soul and captivate the eye.
Sixty-nine kinds of birds, I'm told, including
partridges, thrushes, magpies, warblers, jays,
most feasting on the bounty of the fruit trees.
A nightingale warbles in a golden cage.

The foreground shows the cultivated garden,
contained by a lattice fence and low stone wall.
Beyond, a wild grove boasts oak and laurel;
the date palms mix with cypress, spruce, and pines,
with fruiting quince and pomegranate trees.
Viburnums grow with poppies and acanthus.
All seasons merge; all bloom concurrently—
harmonious as Rome's Augustan Age.

As we reclined on couches piled with cushions,
the servants filled the tables with camel heels,
flamingo's tongues. And then there were the dormice:
first dipped in honey, rolled in poppy seeds.
Exotic dishes I had never seen.
(The silver wine cups featured Dionysus.)
Though we began at five, the courses flowed
as constant as the Tiber through the night.

For entertainment, female slaves who danced
to melodies of lyres, flutes, and harps.
The acrobats and mimes astonished all.
At last it was my turn to play a part
when I was asked to read my poetry.
I saw the empress smile as I took my bow.

Take care so that you are well, my friend,
                Cornelius

Note: Cura ut valeas (Take care so that you are well) *was a common closing to Latin letters.*

Detto

> *The Italian word* detto *means* known as *and was used to introduce the nicknames of 13th- to 17th-century Italian artists.*

Not their names but what they're called:
Girolamo Mazzola, the little one from Parma,
detto Parmigianino;
swarthy-skinned Agnolo di Cosimo,
detto Bronzino;
Jacopo Comin, the dyer's son,
detto Tintoretto.

Nicknames usurped given names,
as they do now:
Magic Johnson, *Babe* Ruth, *Lady Day*.
Children coin cruel names:
four-eyes, beanpole, stinky, tubs,
but also *Yogi,* lovingly bestowed
by friends on my catcher-husband, Lawrence.

Then there are names reserved for family:
sibling names shaped by a toddler's tongue
(*Daisy* for *David, Sa* for Melissa),
pet names tossed between husband and wife
(often embarrassing to hear),
old-world names for new-world grandmas
(nana, nonna, oma, abuela).
Passwords for insiders,
who alone can tell the story.

The Day Verrocchio Put His Paintbrush Down

Andrea del Verrocchio's Renaissance workshop in Florence included, at one time or another, Botticelli, Perugino, Ghirlandaio, di Credi, and Leonardo da Vinci. Leonardo was an apprentice in 1466 at 14 and later became an assistant until he left in 1473. Vasari said that after Verrocchio saw the angel that Leonardo had painted in Verrocchio's Baptism of Christ, *he vowed never to paint again and turned to sculpture. This may be apocryphal, but it's a good story. The painting is in Florence's Uffizi Gallery.*

Mine is, indeed, the finest workshop in Florence.
So many have bloomed beneath my watchful eyes:
di Credi, Perugino, Ghirlandaio,
the boy of dazzling skill—Leonardo da Vinci.
I taught him drawing, drafting, modelling, painting.
Later, he added to my *Baptism of Christ*
the beautiful blonde angel on the left.
His use of color and lighting is sublime.
In truth, my passion always has been sculpture.
I trained as a goldsmith, even took the name
of Giuliano Verrocchi, worthy mentor.
I learned to paint with Fra Filippo Lippi,
but sculpture always drew my hands and heart.
The Medicis selected me to craft
the tomb of Cosimo the Elder, founding
patriarch of a dynasty. So grand
my floor design, it won the sacred place
in front of the high altar in San Lorenzo.
A double sepulcher for his two sons:

white marble, porphyry, green serpentine
and bronze acanthus leaves that climbed and flowed.
It was declared to be *a wonder of the world.*
I say my David will rival Donatello's.
And when I finish casting "Christ and St. Thomas"
to occupy a niche in Orsanmichele,[*]
my name will soar in Florence and beyond.
Leave painting to the gifted Leonardo,
Verrocchio will shape the realm of bronze.

---

[*] *Originally an oratory in the monastery of San Michele, Orsanmichele was rebuilt several times. It was built again in 1337 to market and store grain. It eventually became a church with fourteen exterior niches for religious statues paid for by the principal guilds of Florence. Some of the artists, besides Verrocchio, who contributed during the Renaissance were Donatello, Ghiberti, and Luca della Robbia.*

The Perfect Gentleman

In 1515, Raphael finished an oil portrait of Count Baldassare Castiglione, the author of The Courtier *(1528), when Castiglione was 37. Among Raphael's most famous portraits, it is in the Louvre.*

How every inch the courtier is this Count,
who wrote the book on protocol. His clothes
and poised demeanor are impeccable:
black doublet wrapped in fine gray fur, the bloused
white pleated shirt beneath. And on his head,
which to his shame was bald, good taste confirmed:
black turban topped by a grand black notched beret.
A courtier to nobles first, he rose
to be ambassador to Rome, unmatched
as tightrope walker of diplomacy.
And yet the viewer cannot help but note
a weary melancholy in his eyes.
Perhaps because the painter was his friend,
the Count allowed a glint of truth to show—
after twenty years of service, the cost
of knowing what a courtier must do.

Water Games

During the Renaissance and after, the Italian aristocracy loved to show off the extravagant gardens of their country villas. One of their amusements was to soak their guests with hidden jets of water (giochi d'acqua). Owned by Cosimo I, Grand Duke of Tuscany, The Medici Villa Reale at Castello hid a famous one.

1569, The Grotto of the Animals, the Medici Villa at Castello

The Noblewoman

This Tuscan heat—I'm broiling like a sirloin.
Perhaps this grotto will afford relief.
The walls boast such a beautiful design
of pebbles, sea shells, mosaics on the walls.
Three fountains: two white marble, one in peach.
Above them a menagerie in stone—
giraffe, wild boar, an elephant and bear,
a camel, antelope, rhinoceros—
a unicorn for fancy. And so cool . . .
What was that click? The gates have locked us in.
Where is this water spouting from? The floor!
My dress, the green cut-velvet one, is drenched.
My hair, which just this morning Anna dressed
with fine gold net and precious stones, is dripping.
Is this the Grand Duke's version of a joke?
I must laugh like the others (Oh, my shoes!).

The Nobleman

Last time my cloak took seven days to dry,
so this time I picked out a lighter one.
Of course I kept the secret, as the Grand Duke
cautioned—*There is no joke without surprise.*
I'm soaked to my silk chemise. My wide-brimmed black
felt hat is weighed down by its sodden fur.

Look at Umberto, searching fruitlessly
for refuge from the spray. We must appear
like living sculptures trapped in one of the fountains.
See how Rosina tries to brush the water
from her brocade gown. Surely the silk is ruined—
and yet, she may be asked to come again.

Cosimo I de' Medici, Grand Duke of Tuscany

Delightful, how they scurry. No escape.
Just like my conquest of Siena, but
with water flowing now, not blood. I like
to watch their actions: first the shock, then aimless
darting about—resignation and defeat.
At first, they toured my gardens, grandly done
by Tribolo, with statues of my family's
revered virtues: justice, wisdom—and so on;
then terracotta pots of citrus trees,
so large the gardeners had to wheel them into
the limonaia against the winter freeze.
The grotto gates have opened now; my guests
repair to their rooms to change their clothes and rest.
It's time for me to take my rest as well,
remembering my Eleonora, taken
as well as two of my sons, two of my daughters.
I'll spend my waning days here at Castello,
survey my woods and gardens, count the lemons
perfuming the air. There still is time for laughter.

Tour Guide's Lament

Florence, Italy, 2015

I lead my flock, who ceaselessly complain
about the coffee, crowds, the bus, the heat.
With haloed smile I comfort, and explain

that pasta is *al dente* here, domain
of Chianti, white bean soup, and wine-braised meat.
I school my flock, whose taste is so mundane.

Raising my crook—red banner on a cane—
I point out Brunelleschi's dome. They tweet.
With hollow smile I linger to explain

the scaffold-free support built to maintain
that massive weight. They only want to eat.
I tolerate my flock, their sour refrain

that Tuscan bread is tasteless, that the rain
is forming channels on the cobbled street.
With frozen smile, I struggle to explain

that since the ancient tax, bakers abstain
from salt, and that the dewy air is sweet.
I loathe my flock: they trigger a migraine.
With twisted smile, I lecture through the pain.

Like Wingless Birds

A Modest Proposal

*In Renaissance Italy (and even before),
luxury or sumptuary laws were imposed to restrict
extravagance in dress and social behavior.*

When Venice published Sumptuary Laws,
the nobles were aghast. How to parade
one's station lacking velvet and brocade?
And how to tell the eagles from the daws?
We need such legislation now because
of reigning plutocrats, who are afraid
that every protest is an ambuscade.
We need an edict that will give them pause.

I offer not admonishment but tweaks:
raccoon instead of sable, cheap Bordeaux,
nine-karat gold with zircons, no antiques,
three bathrooms in a penthouse, escargot
with beans instead of cognac, roasted leeks.
So simple to improve the status quo.

The Whole Truth

Truth consists in some form of correspondence between belief and fact.
—Bertrand Russell, "Truth and Falsehood"
in *Problems of Philosophy* (1912)

Since when is wish as gold as fact?
Conviction true if never tried?
Opinion sound if never backed
by data that are verified?

Judgment

The shabby man enters our subway car.
No life, he begins, *especially for children—
a shelter is no shelter for a child.
Mine are six and three; their mother is dead.*

He offers a plastic cup as he moves slowly,
left leg slightly dragging.
My eight-year-old grandson stares
while his mother and I look away.

Our stop stops his pitch,
but my grandson's downcast face
follows us to the street.

The Battered Wife

At least my hair will hide the purple bruise
below my ear. I'm best in winter, time
for turtlenecks, long-sleeves, and woolen scarves.
I'll say I tripped on the hallway rug again;
another bathtub accident won't do.
Did Johnny hear me scream when the dishes crashed?
Is Katie in the closet with her bear?
We'll go to Helen's house; she understands.
He used to be so gentle, almost boyish,
stroking my hair, calling me *little girl*.
The children came, and I kept gaining weight
(mustn't forget the vitamins and toys).
Mom says that marriage is a bramble bush
with berries for the picking (*learn to live
with scratches*). These are more than scratches—still,
the fruit is irresistible (and sweet).
I'll stay at Helen's while we all calm down.
He'll call, crying, promise me the world,
but I'll be firm—hold off for one more day.
It will be different this time. I feel sure.

Turquoise Anita on the Dance Floor

For Anita Dorn

Black hair flying, you fling your arms and twirl
to gypsy strains, your billowing dress as turquoise
as your eyes. When waiters stare at you, we smile.
Years fall away—it's 1939—
and you, a student from Estonia,
are summering in carefree, war-free Finland.
In 1940, the last year in your homeland,
you meet Alyosha, a Soviet sailor with hair
as blond as wheat. He saves you from the Russian
trucks that doom the deported to Siberia.
This is the first of your cat lives, all of them needed.
As Soviet tanks usurp the streets of Tallinn,
you lose your house, move in with Uncle Hans;
suitcases line the walls like honeycombs.
Friends disappear—the family moves again;
your journey into homelessness begins.

Southern Germany, 1941,
you live in Werneck's gilded archbishop's palace,
sardined with thousands of other refugees.
Children, peasants, riffraff, pampered ladies—
all fighting for scraps of cheese that walk away
on maggots. Daily fights and daily curses.
Yet there are evenings in the Himmelssahl—
painted clouds on the ceiling, velvet drapes,
a grand piano played by artists in rags.

Swept to Poland, in 1944,
you share a heatless apartment; greedy old man
reserves his small coal ration for himself.
On Christmas night you find the church door locked
to keep the heat and swollen crowds inside.
Returning to your icy nest, you hear,

Come in, Ninotschka from your Siberian neighbor,
who spites the war with piroshkies, herrings, bacon,
chocolates, cakes, a puffing samovar.
And blessed heat: a fat, potbellied stove.
You sleep there, at its feet—a Christmas gift.

Weeks later, Russian artillery creeps closer;
you join an endless westward line, trudging
with feisty Dora, from Berlin, who kicks you
awake when you fall, exhausted, into the snow.
A trail of frozen bodies lines the roadside.

You land at Wurzburg's Cloister Oberzell,
half a straw sleeping bag against the cold.
Officially dead without papers—no food stamps—
the menu, bread crusts and salted potato peels.
A nun puts newspaper caps on shivering tulip
sprouts to save them from the frost, as Wurzburg
like her sister, Dresden, smokes in ruins.

A lifetime later, you make a pilgrimage,
returning to Tallinn in 1996.
Gray and shabby, paint peeling and chimneys crumbling,
the thousand-year-old city is being redressed.
Construction crews demolish the frail wooden houses
while disco music strikes the ancient walls.
Still standing are her medieval ramparts,
tall towers, peaked tile roofs, and linden trees.
Still dazzling, Catherine the Great's pink summer palace,
Peter the Great's hunting lodge. But you are
an outsider now, stray cat searching for home.

Your memories rise and fall like ocean swells:
Estonia, Finland, Poland, Germany.
Flames and frostbite, bread crusts and tulip sprouts.
But always, in my memory book, you chase
away the ghosts in yards of turquoise silk,
dancing, defiantly, the steps of life.

Waiting for the Open Air in a Time of Covid

O welche Lust, in freier Luft
Den Atem leicht zu heben!
Oh what joy, in the open air
Freely to breathe again!
   —The Prisoners' Chorus from Beethoven's opera *Fidelio*

Let out from cells as sunless as the grave,
political prisoners shuffle toward the light.
Brief respite, but the famished souls behave
like wingless birds still contemplating flight.

The beauty of the music underscores
the fragile gift of freedom. (I always cry.)
One voice sings hope and faith in God, ignores
the fact that they are watched with ear and eye.

Though self-imposed, our prison has its bars—
if only made of linen or of lace—
on windows that divide us from the stars
and frame a grandchild's disappointed face.

As hostages to loneliness, we need
to hear the harmony of being freed.

Staccato of the Cane

At Home When Old

June 2020

This plague enshrouds me,
numbs my sensibilities
as I languish in my safe cocoon.
Yet my heart still aches for
the death of another black man
when a white policeman presses a knee
on a human neck.
Youthful faces protest:
impatient, immortal, immune,
except to batons and pepper spray.
I'd like to march
as I did in 1969
against the war in Vietnam,
but my legs won't support me.
I'm just an observer—
watching, always watching.

Mind to Body

Let's fine-tune our partnership.
I'll devise plans for fighting decline—
perhaps a piano or meditation class.
You can rouse muscle memory,
quiet overactive nerves,
shower me with endorphins when I exercise.
Yeah, yeah, we aren't twenty anymore.

I'll renounce bike riding,
weeding my garden,
carrying packages in both arms.
But I would like to sit through an act of *Don Giovanni,*
then walk to the bathroom and wait on the line.
Or examine paintings at a museum under my own steam.
I knew exactly what you were going to say.

About my balance—
I've gotten good at falling,
so I'm reading about how to land properly.
I love the part about relaxing
so that muscles aren't tense:
pivoting to the side and protecting the head,
aiming to fall on a fleshy part (which one?),
not on the hands.
All this supposes presence of mind, obedient body.
Give me a break. No, forget that.
Could we argue how to solve this after lunch?

Cane People

Where were they hiding before I broke my hip?
I see them everywhere: in shops and parks,
in pharmacies and doctors' offices.
I wince watching them climb the subway stairs,
scale buses while the riders wait or help,
extract themselves from cars in heavy traffic,
attempt to carve a space in callous crowds.
And always the soft staccato of the cane,
tapping the code of injury or age,
conveyed to members of the clique, who may
return the secret signal with a smile.

My Last School Reunion

Big Bernie steers his walker—now we know;
Jean's sensible shoes insult her stylish dress;
Fred lost his winning smile some years ago,
but Bella is still pretty, more or less.

They laugh about sarcastic Mrs. J,
who tortured only boys in English class—
about the stuttering of Mr. K,
who always let the weakest students pass.

I recollect the bullies, how they led
poor Robby to an overdose at home,
the way the cool girls whispered, head-to-head,
while Lorna ate her salad all alone.

They sing old songs, try to recall a name,
share smartphone apps. I don't know why I came.

Traveling

Where are the days of serendipity,
when plans were flexible, and so were we?
When one of us could climb up Giotto's Tower—
when both, like Holland's tulips, were in flower.
Now all is measured by our drops and pills
(for wayward heartbeats and digestive ills).
We know the nearest hospital address
and where to go in case of tooth distress.
We locate bathrooms in hotel or bar,
park benches when our destination's far.
Our hearing's good except for when it's not;
we can't remember what we just forgot.
We smile at each new day and hope that chance will.
(We have insurance if we need to cancel.)

The Club

I've just been told that I am in.
No sponsor is required, no dues.
(The shock was followed by the blues.)
All questions asked—a single answer:
My membership card says *breast cancer*.

Although I'm not known as a joiner,
I have a new community
as well as a new glossary:
carcinoma, sentinel, node,
passwords to a private code.

No blackballing in this club.
All are admitted (none decline),
hoping for clearance to resign,
cradling the wish to be benign.

Let-Down

How strange, when old,
to think about nursing my baby.
A need to nurture again,
to see my milk turn into flesh?
I still can feel the tingling *let-down*
as the cells released milk.
At first the baby's sucking
caused the milk to come.
Later, the cry alone
propelled the flow.

Why summon this now?
The cancer began
in the milk duct of the breast.
An irony to live by.

While You're Away

For my husband on the eve of his surgery

While you're away I'll shun the rose,
the cool night-breeze that sweetly blows,
the trilling of the cardinal's song.
Somehow it suddenly seems wrong
to revel when the pleasure goes.

And yet my tree hydrangea grows
with daily confidence. Who knows?
Perhaps I also can be strong
while you're away.

Without your buoyant smile that shows
the spirit of the man I chose,
without your often off-key song
that strives for Wagner (not too long),
I'll mimic coping, I suppose,
while you're away.

Being Read To

Every night my husband reads to me
in bed to usher me to sleep.
Often, books about Italy, but never poetry.
Too hard, he says, *I'd have to rehearse.*
So I hear about Verdi's operas,
especially his last one, *Falstaff,*
a comedy he wrote when he was almost 80.
About *Domus Aurea,*
the Roman Palace of Emperor Nero—
hundreds of rooms,
covered with gold leaf and frescoes.
Raphael and Michelangelo
were let down shafts to see
this buried exhibition of excess.
About the Villa d'Este in Tivoli, near Rome,
its 16th-century gardens and dazzling fountains,
fueled by gravity instead of pumps.
The Organ Fountain, recently restored,
once more plays spurts of music as the water flows.
All with pictures that quicken memory.
This reading has long been a ritual.
Not like a parent lulling a child,
chasing away cares or monster fears.
Not like Cupid leaving Psyche in the dark.
More like partners sharing, then parting
without sorrow or regret,
in the hope of awakening
together in the morning light.

Metamorphosis

Whenever I see Daphne's toes
begin to root in marble soil,
her fingers leafing from Apollo's
grasp, which makes her flesh recoil,

I realize that change is good
—not only to ward off advances—
and, like a sudden legacy, should
invigorate one's circumstances.

The rules say there is no reversing
a classical identity,
no trying-on and no rehearsing,
so I must find one meant for me.

Not Echo, with her borrowed voice
(I interrupt—it would be fair),
or Arethusa's spring (bad choice—
damp weather gives me frizzy hair).

Nor Io, who could not escape
when Juno's gadfly wrecked her life.
Not even Galatea's shape
would lure me to the sculptor's knife.

On second thought, I think I'll wait—
applying at the final stroke—
for Baucis and Philemon's fate:
a linden mingled with his oak.

About the Author

Carolyn Raphael retired from the English Department at Queensborough Community College, CUNY, after more than thirty years of teaching. Her poems have appeared in journals and anthologies, including *Blue Unicorn, Mezzo Cammin, Oberon,* and *Verse Daily.* Seven of her poems were translated into Italian by Luigi Bonafini and edited by Michael Palma for the *Journal of Italian Translation,* Spring, 2019.

Her chapbook *Diagrams of Bittersweet* was published by Somers Rocks Press in 1997, and her poetry collection *The Most Beautiful Room in the World* was published by David Robert Books in 2010. Her collection *Dancing with Bare Feet* was published by Kelsay Books/White Violet Press in 2016, and her chapbook *Grandma Poems—Not Too Sweet* was published by Kelsay Books/Aldrich Press in 2017.

Carolyn Raphael is the poetry coordinator of Great Neck Plaza in Great Neck, New York. She created "Poetry in the Plaza," which places a poem each month on local bulletin boards and on the village website. She also coordinates the annual Great Neck Plaza Poetry Contest.

www.ingramcontent.com/pod-product-compliance
Lightning Source LLC
Chambersburg PA
CBHW030912170426
43193CB00009BA/820